NEW VANGUARD 234

BRITISH GUIDED MISSILE DESTROYERS

County-class, Type 82, Type 42 and Type 45

EDWARD HAMPSHIRE   ILLUSTRATED BY PAUL WRIGHT

First published in Great Britain in 2016 by Osprey Publishing,
PO Box 883, Oxford, OX1 9PL, UK
1385 Broadway, 5th Floor, New York, NY 10018, USA
E-mail: info@ospreypublishing.com

Osprey Publishing, part of Bloomsbury Publishing Plc

A CIP catalogue record for this book is available from the British Library

Print ISBN: 978 1 4728 1116 5
PDF ebook ISBN: 978 1 4728 1117 2
ePub ebook ISBN: 978 1 4728 1118 9

Index by Rob Munro
Typeset in Sabon and Myriad Pro
Originated by PDQ Media, Bungay, UK
Printed in China through World Print Ltd

16 17 18 19 20 10 9 8 7 6 5 4 3 2 1

Osprey Publishing supports the Woodland Trust, the UK's leading woodland
conservation charity. Between 2014 and 2018 our donations will be spent
on their Centenary Woods project in the UK.

www.ospreypublishing.com

Imperial War Museums Collections
Many of the photos in this book come from the huge collections of IWM
(Imperial War Museums) which cover all aspects of conflict involving Britain
and the Commonwealth since the start of the twentieth century. These rich
resources are available online to search, browse and buy at www.
iwmcollections.org.uk. In addition to Collections Online, you can visit the
Visitor Rooms where you can explore over 8 million photographs,
thousands of hours of moving images, the largest sound archive of its kind
in the world, thousands of diaries and letters written by people in wartime,
and a huge reference library. To make an appointment, call (020) 7416
5320, or e-mail mail@iwm.org.uk
Imperial War Museums www.iwm.org.uk

CONTENTS

BRITISH GUIDED MISSILE DESTROYERS

COUNTY-CLASS, TYPE 82, TYPE 42 AND TYPE 45

INTRODUCTION

British naval strategy, the air threat and guided missile destroyers

At the end of World War II, with the Axis powers defeated, the British economy and its infrastructure needed to be rebuilt, so spending money on new warships was consequently a low priority. Many ships laid down during the war were either put into reserve soon after completion or their construction was suspended; some unbuilt vessels were even broken up on the shipbuilders' slips.

However, the takeover of Eastern Europe by Soviet-backed communists and evidence that Stalin was investing in new armaments, including submarines, warships and bombers, caused British naval spending to rise. Investment in the emerging technology of anti-aircraft guided missiles began, designs for new frigates and destroyers were developed, and the building of ships, the construction of which had been suspended, was restarted. The Korean War and the explosion of the first Soviet atom bomb increased fears that a war with the Soviets and their allies was imminent, so defence spending increased yet further.

The Soviets had captured German guided-missile and jet-engine technology and were developing their own anti-ship guided missiles. In the last years of World War II, the Germans had developed the ability to pre-programme long-range missiles filled with explosives so that they would hit designated targets. Their accuracy was at best in the region of 6 to 12 miles – this range had been sufficient for the famous 'doodlebug' V1 and V2 aerial raids of 1944 and 1945. The Soviets developed this technology further and by the 1950s guided rockets were able to change their course in mid-flight, a vital pre-requisite for intercepting moving warships. With the earliest missiles, this was done by following a radar beam sent out by the launching aircraft and then, in the final stages of flight, from a radar on the missile itself, thus providing much greater accuracy than the German flying bombs from which they were derived. The first Soviet anti-ship missile, the AS-1 Kennel,

A Tu16 Badger bomber with a single AS-6 Kingfish missile on the port wing. The Kingfish was introduced in 1977 and was carried on both Badger and Backfire bombers. It had a range of up to 350 nautical miles and a speed of over Mach 2.5. (US Navy)

A photograph taken from the hangar of HMS *Glasgow* shows not only her Lynx helicopter secured to the ship's flight deck but also a shadowing Soviet Kresta II class cruiser. (Imperial War Museum, CT 390)

which was about the size of an aircraft and was reportedly based on the MiG 15 jet, appeared in 1958 and was launched from a Badger bomber.

The British Sea Slug missile system was developed to counter Soviet bombers and subsonic aircraft-like missiles such as the Kennel. The Royal Navy planned for a 'second Battle of the Atlantic' in which convoys of US supplies and troops to Europe would have to be protected from Soviet attack by submarine, surface raider, aircraft or guided missile. When it became clear that the Soviet nuclear arsenal was growing, strategy shifted towards fighting a 'broken-backed' war in which naval forces would continue to protect US convoys even after nuclear exchanges had heavily damaged the infrastructure of many NATO states. During this period, design studies for air-defence ships focused on convoy missile escorts: vessels that could be built in some numbers but did not necessarily have the all-round 'fleet capabilities' necessary to operate in naval task forces.

Following the 1957 Defence White Paper, in which it was acknowledged that maintaining a large reserve fleet was no longer viable and that nuclear exchanges would lessen the likelihood of a long-term convoy campaign, the Navy carved out a new strategy for itself as Britain began to withdraw from many of its colonies across the globe. The Soviets and their allies began to involve themselves in conflicts in decolonizing states, while Britain fought a series of 'end-of-empire' wars and insurgencies in Malaya, Kenya, Cyprus, Borneo and Aden. In this context, an 'East of Suez' strategy of worldwide deployment and mixed-capability task forces with a strong focus on capable 'fleet' vessels was developed. The County-class destroyers were one of the main products of this strategic focus. In addition, in the early 1960s the second generation of long-range Soviet missiles entered service, including long-range anti-ship missiles such as the AS-2 Kipper, the AS-5 Kelt and the ship-launched SS-N-3 Shaddock missile. Shorter-range missiles such as the SS-N-2 Styx also entered service. The Silkworm, a Chinese variant of the Styx, appeared in the 1970s. The British Sea Dart missile system was developed from the early 1960s onwards to deal with these new, relatively small, supersonic or near-supersonic high-altitude missiles.

By the mid-1960s the cost of the 'East of Suez' strategy caused a number of expensive defence programmes to be cancelled, including the CVA01 strike aircraft carrier. The Type 82 destroyer, the first ship to carry the Sea Dart missile system, had become the main air-defence escort for the carrier, so its cancellation meant that only one of the class was built. There followed a few years of strategic flux in which the 'East of Suez' strategy theoretically remained in place, but many of the weapon systems to maintain it had been cancelled and the political will to continue such a world role was diminishing. In this vacuum, the Type 42 destroyer was developed as a cheaper ship to get as many Sea Dart air-defence missile systems to sea as quickly as possible. By 1968, after the Type 42 design had already been agreed, British naval strategy returned to a focus on the eastern Atlantic and a potential convoy war, lasting only a couple of days or weeks, against Soviet forces in a period of increasing tension before a possible nuclear exchange. Conflicts other than direct confrontation with the Soviets in the eastern Atlantic were now considered to be less likely.

The late 1970s saw a leap in Soviet capabilities with the introduction of the supersonic Backfire bomber, which carried the Mach 2.5 AS-4 Kitchen or AS-6 Kingfish missiles and could be deployed in 'regimental' massed saturation attacks which could overwhelm a Type 42 destroyer. Designs such

as the Type 43, Type 44 and the NFR90 were developed which would have a greater capacity to withstand such attacks.

Despite the Falklands War, which highlighted the threat from sea-skimming anti-ship missiles such as Exocet, overall British naval strategy did not change significantly until the Soviet retreat from Eastern Europe and the collapse of the Soviet Union in 1989–91. From this time until the Strategic Defence Review of 1998, an 'expeditionary warfare' strategy was developed – with echoes of the 'East of Suez' strategy forty years earlier – in which British forces could be deployed globally to support peacekeeping, humanitarian intervention, defend British interests and, from 2001, to help fight the global 'war on terror'. In this context the Horizon project and Type 45 destroyers were developed. The Type 45 finally enabled the Royal Navy to counter saturation attacks and complex threat environments, and perhaps even undertake theatre ballistic missile defence.

In spite of these shifts in strategy, which suggested the need for different force mixes and types of vessels, the increased length of design development and procurement has meant that British air-defence destroyers have had to be flexible and adaptable warships, capable of many roles and able to be repeatedly updated over their increasingly long service lives.

WEAPONS AND SYSTEMS

Countering the air threat

The British, in common with the United States, developed two types of air-defence missile systems in the 1940s and 1950s. The first type, medium-range 'area defence' systems that can defend a number of vessels and not just the ship that the system is on, was developed using innovations from World War II Allied and Axis scientists, such as the German V1 and V2 guided rockets. Area defence is a complex task as it requires a missile to intercept a target that might be flying past it, rather than one flying straight towards it. A large, medium- or long-range missile would therefore be needed, with sophisticated ship-based and missile-based systems and radar to detect and track the target and then guide the missile onto that target. Detection and tracking would be undertaken by air-search radar in aircraft or on board ship, while the fire-control radar for the missile system would 'lock on' to the target, and then help guide the missile to the target. The area-defence missile would often have its own homing capability for the final stages before interception.

The second type of air-defence system is the short-range 'point defence' system, which in effect replaced the capability of ships' short-range anti-aircraft

A Sea Cat launcher being loaded. Unlike the complex below-decks loading system of the Sea Slug and Sea Dart, Sea Cat was manually loaded by crew members. This resulted in minimal impact on the design and structure of warships, but did mean that crew were vulnerable to the elements and to enemy action. (MoD Naval Historical Branch)

guns. Sea Cat was the first such point-defence anti-aircraft and anti-missile system, although its range of just 3 miles meant that it could only defend the ship from which it was fired, and was a system that would intercept the enemy with only seconds to go before impact. It also had a very limited capability against supersonic targets, and early versions required manual above-decks guidance to the target. However, Sea Cat proved successful, and was in service with the Royal Navy from 1960 to the 1990s and, consequently, was adopted by the navies of several other countries. The County-class destroyers were each fitted with two Sea Cat systems, each either side of the ship's hangar. The successor to the Sea Cat was Sea Wolf, which was fitted to a number of British frigates between 1980 and the 2000s. Much updated, it is still in Royal Navy service today. It was much more effective at

A Sea Slug firing from a County-class destroyer. Sea Slug was unique in that its four booster rockets were wrapped around the front of the missile, not the rear. (MoD Naval Historical Branch)

intercepting supersonic targets, but was still a short-range point-defence system unable to defend other vessels from attack (as was confirmed in the Falklands). Plans to fit BAC's lightweight Sea Wolf launchers to Batch 3 Type 42 destroyers were dropped in 1990, a few months before the first planned installation.

Sea Slug

The first British area-defence missile system was Sea Slug, designed by Armstrong Whitworth. Its development began in the last few months of World War II, but costs and complexity were severely underestimated and the missile and its system did not enter full service until 1961. Sea Slug had a range of 30,000 yards with a maximum altitude of 55,000 feet. The Sea Slug guidance radar, the Type 901, both tracked the target and guided the missile towards it. Because Sea Slug did not have its own homing capacity, guidance was less accurate the further away the target was, and the missile 'rode' the

beam of the guidance radar to take it to its target. The missiles were stowed horizontally in a hangar-like structure below decks but above the waterline. Sea Slug Mk 1 was fitted to the trials ship *Girdle Ness* and to the first four County-class destroyers described on page 18.

A modified Sea Slug system (Mk 2) was fitted to the second batch of County-class destroyers. Target selection in the ships' operations room was semi-automated with only the decision to fire being made by an operations-room officer; this system – ADAWS (Action Data Automation Weapon System) – was the first of its kind installed in a Royal Navy vessel. Sea Slug Mk 2 also had an increased range of 49,000 yards and maximum altitude of 65,000 feet. By the Falklands conflict Sea Slug was obsolescent and was not used for air defence. However, Sea Slug missiles were used for rough-and-ready shore bombardment.

Sea Dart

The Sea Dart system was originally developed by Hawker Siddeley and built by British Aerospace in the 1960s as a lightweight alternative to Sea Slug for fitting on frigate-sized hulls. It soon became clear that it would become a successor to Sea Slug itself. Early requirements were for a missile that could engage high-altitude Mach 3 targets at a range of 30,000 yards and a maximum altitude of 65,000 feet. Sea Dart was a much faster missile than Sea Slug and the system had two guidance radars, so it was much more capable of engaging multiple targets in succession. The missile itself also had a homing capability, with sensors able to home in on a target 'illuminated' by the launching ship's guidance radar.

This image of the Sea Dart launcher on HMS *Edinburgh* shows its twin arms and the blast doors below from which the missiles emerge. The missiles on the launcher are red, denoting their test/exercise status. (MoD/Open Government Licence v3.0)

Unlike Sea Slug, the missiles were stored in a magazine close to the waterline and brought upwards by chain hoist, warmed up, and taken above decks through blast doors onto a twin-arm launcher. Sea Dart first entered service on board the only Royal Navy Type 82 destroyer, HMS *Bristol*, and then in the Type 42 destroyers, or Sheffield class, with a scaled-down launcher and smaller missile magazine. The Type 42s were originally designed with single-arm launchers, but these were modified early in the design process to twin-arm. Sea Dart in box launchers was proposed by their manufacturer, British Aerospace, in 1978 but none was ever purchased by the Royal Navy or by other navies. Sea Dart was updated progressively through the 1980s and 1990s: guidance was improved, a new warhead was added and new fusing was also included.

Sea Viper

During the 1990s the Royal Navy pursued a collaborative warship project – Horizon – with France and Italy to replace the Type 42 destroyers. The Horizon frigate and its fate is described in more detail on page 34, but when the United Kingdom made the decision to back out of the project, it retained the tri-nation Aster 15 and Aster 30 missiles that were being developed for the Horizon local area defence and full area defence respectively, as well as the Sylver vertical launch system. Together with the Sampson multi-function radar and MBDA's PAAMS (Principal Anti-Air Missile System) command-and-control system, these make up the Sea Viper area-defence missile system that has been fitted to the Type 45 destroyers. The Sampson radar is said to have a range of almost 250 miles and the ability to track hundreds of targets simultaneously. There are six eight-cell Sylver launcher modules on each Type 45, each capable of taking either the medium-range Aster 15 (18-mile) missile or the long-range Aster 30 (75-mile) missile. The ship's command-and-control systems are able to direct at least ten missiles simultaneously and send target-position updates to Aster

OPPOSITE

Antrim at sea in 1975 showing her aft weapon systems and sensors to good effect. Forward of the twin-arm Sea Slug launcher is the flight deck with a Wessex on deck. Forward of that is the large Type 901 radar. Abreast the Type 901 can be seen the starboard Sea Cat launcher, its Type 904 fire control above. Below the large 'double bedstead' Type 965 air-search radar is the Type 278 height finder. (MoD Naval Historical Branch)

A Wessex landing on the flight deck of HMS *Devonshire*. The County class were the first ships smaller than an aircraft carrier to take a helicopter of this size. (MoD Naval Historical Branch)

missiles in flight. At the final stage before impact, Aster's own radar guides the missile to its destination. The combination of Sampson and the Aster 30 long-range missile, in addition to the linked command-and-control systems, give the Type 45 an area air defence capability well in advance of the local area defence capability of the Franco-Italian Horizon ships that were eventually built.

Other weapon systems

Although the 'main armament' and raison d'être of the guided missile destroyer was air defence, such vessels have had considerable general-purpose capabilities. Anti-submarine warfare was revolutionized in the post-war period: submarines could attack from under the water, had a much greater subsurface speed, and by the 1960s large numbers of nuclear-powered boats had been built by the Soviets. Submarines were no longer surface torpedo boats that could dive underwater for relatively short periods to avoid detection, they were now true 'submarines' that could patrol underwater for weeks and months and fire their weapons from under the sea. In response to this threat, traditional anti-submarine mortars were supplemented and replaced by a number of weapon systems. The first of these were torpedo-armed helicopters: either engaging targets using sensor information from their parent ship, such as Wasp and Lynx helicopters, or using sonar-buoys and dipping sonars on board the helicopter itself, such as the Wessex, Sea King and Merlin helicopters. The second was a guided-missile system used to deliver a torpedo quickly to its target: the Australian Ikara was fitted to a number of British frigates as well as to the Royal Navy Type 82. Finally, in the early 1980s British warships were fitted with STWS anti-submarine torpedo launchers in triple tubes as a shipborne defence against submarines. These and later torpedo tubes have been fitted to Type 42 and Type 45 destroyers. Towards the end of the careers of the Type 42s the tubes were generally removed because of top-weight problems.

For anti-surface warfare, British guided missile destroyers have been fitted with twin 4.5-inch guns in Mark 6 mountings (County class) and a single 4.5-inch gun in a Mark 8 mounting (Type 42, Type 82, Type 45). The Mark 6 mounting was developed towards the end of World War II and was the standard British medium gun mounting until the 1970s. It had a rate of fire of 24 rounds a minute and could elevate to 80 degrees for the anti-aircraft role. The Mark 8 replaced the Mark 6 in 1973. It was fully automatic, had a rate of 25 rounds a minute but had a lower elevation of 55 degrees. Both guns and mountings were used successfully for shore bombardment in the Falklands War. In addition, ships' helicopters were fitted with small anti-ship missiles to deal with fast attack craft and patrol vessels, such as the Sea Skua missile system on the Lynx helicopter. The four Batch 2 County-class destroyers were also fitted with launchers for four Exocet sea-skimming anti-ship missiles in place of their second 4.5-inch twin mounting. The Type 45s have been fitted to take the US Harpoon anti-ship missile system, but so far only HMS *Diamond* and HMS *Duncan* have been so fitted.

Following the Falklands War it was clear that British naval vessels needed a last-ditch point-defence system to supplement Sea Wolf and Sea Dart against anti-ship missiles. The US Phalanx radar-guided rapid-fire rotary cannon system aims to destroy a missile in the final stages of its flight with 20mm automatic fire, although the risk of debris from a destroyed missile crashing into a ship remains in some instances. The Phalanx was fitted to all surviving Type 42 destroyers after the conflict and has also been fitted to the Type 45 destroyers.

All British destroyers have been fitted with a range of light weapons of between 20mm and 40mm calibre. Before the Falklands War, two such weapons were usually fitted either side amidships – for tasks for which a 4.5-inch gun would be excessive. Immediately after the conflict the role played by these additional light weapons in the constrained environment of San Carlos water and around the coast of the Falklands was recognized. Many such weapons were therefore placed aboard the surviving County-class Type 82 and Type 42 destroyers until the Phalanx was installed.

Sensors, command and communication systems

The revolution in guided missile air defence would not have been possible without the use of radars to detect and track aircraft and missiles before they are visible to the naked eye, and then to guide missiles onto their target once launched. The picture of the battlespace that radar provides to tactical command systems enables such systems to undertake the processing required to evaluate and select targets for engagement, and help calculate the required timings and directions for missile launch.

HMS *Fife* following the fitting of the Exocet missiles. Racks for Exocet canisters can be seen aft of the twin 4.5-inch mounting. Two canisters have been added starboard with the two port racks left empty. (MoD Naval Historical Branch)

Radar	Type	Fitted on
Long-range air-search radars: these scan outwards over a long range to detect targets as far out as possible.	Type 965 (AKE I)	County-class Batch 1
	Type 965 (AKE II)	County-class Batch 2, Type 82, Type 42 Batch 1
	Type 1022	Type 42, Batches 2 and 3, modernized Batch 1 and Type 82
	Type 1046 (S1850M)	Type 45
Medium-range target designation/ surveillance radars: these radars then pick up the targets identified by the search radar for designation/prioritization. They can also have medium-range search capability.	Type 992	County-class Batch 1
	Type 992Q/R	County-class Batch 2, Type 82, Type 42
	Type 996	Modernized Type 42
	Type 1045 (Sampson)	Type 45 (surveillance/fire control)
	Type 1048	Type 45 (surface search)
Height-finding radars: these supplemented the above radars in the County class.	Type 277Q	County-class Batch 1
	Type 278	County-class Batch 2
Tracking/fire-control radars: receiving the target from the designation radars, these radars 'lock' onto the target, the missile is launched and the radar guides it to the target.	Type 901	County class – Sea Slug
	Type 903	County class – 4.5-inch
	Type 262	County-class Batch 1 – Sea Cat
	Type 904	County-class Batch 2, Batch 1 modernized – Sea Cat
	Type 909	Type 82, Type 42 – Sea Dart
	Type 1045 (Sampson)	Type 45
Navigation radars	Type 978	County class, Type 82
	Type 1006	Type 42
	Type 1007	Modernized Type 42
	Type 1008	Modernized Type 42
	Type 1047	Type 45

Guided missile destroyers are not generally specialist anti-submarine vessels (although the Type 82, HMS *Bristol* had an effective capability), but all have carried active sonars. These send out acoustic pulses which if reflected off a surface and returned to the sender suggest the presence of a submarine or other underwater object. Some, such as the Type 162M, were narrow-beam sonars for detecting submarines on the seabed. Others, such as the Type 184M, had a range of 6,000 yards on a ship travelling 18 knots and were designed to pick up approaching torpedoes or close submarines. The Type 184M was superseded by the Type 2016 and then by the Type 2050. The Type 45 destroyer is fitted with the Type 2091 sonar, a next-generation system that succeeded the Type 2050.

Electronic warfare has been increasingly important in naval warfare since the 1960s. This can take different forms; the three main types are set out in the table opposite. During the 1990–91 Gulf War the electronic warfare weapons fits of the Type 42s – particularly their intercept equipment – proved more capable at detecting incoming threats than their radars, and their effectiveness meant that Type 42s were given full control of electronic warfare in naval operations in the Gulf.

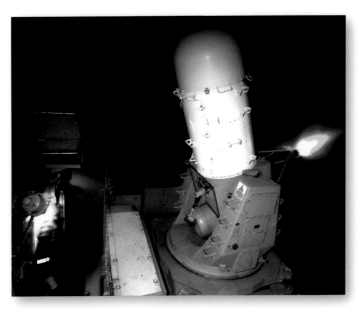

The Vulcan Phalanx close-in weapon system firing from HMS *Southampton* at night in 2005. (MoD/Open Government Licence v3.0)

Electronic warfare	Type	Fitted on
Intercepts: these detect and identify the radars of approaching aircraft, ships and missiles.	UA8/9 (Porker)	County class
	UAA1 (Abbey Hill)	Type 82, Type 42 from 1978
	UAA2	Type 42 by 1990s
	UAT	Type 42, Type 45
Jammers: these jam the radars of approaching missiles. See also DLH decoy outfit below.	Type 669	County class
	Type 670	Type 42, Type 82 post-Falklands
	Type 675 (Guardian)	Type 42 in late 1980s, removed by late 1990s
Decoys: these divert missiles by creating false signals, by firing 'chaff' (metal foil), parachute decoys/jammers (DLH), or floating decoys (DLF).	DLC (Corvus)	Type 42, retrofitted to Counties and Type 82
	DLD: US Mk 36/Mk 137	Type 42
	DLA, DLB, DLJ (Sea Gnat)	Type 42
	DLK (Barricade)	Type 42 (on Armilla patrol)
	DLF (Rubber Duck)	Type 42, Type 45
	DLH (Siren)	Type 42, Type 45
Torpedo decoys and defence systems	Type 182	County class, Type 82, Type 42
	Type 2070	Type 42 by 2000s
	Type 2170	Type 45 (fitted for – but not with)

Tactical command systems were first developed to cope with the tracking and interception of multiple targets, initially in the air, but subsequently also on the surface and below it. The first systems were primarily manual with analogue calculating support and were installed in carriers. In the first batch of County-class destroyers targets were selected manually using selection aids; however, in the second batch the ADAWS 1 tactical command system was trialled. This system automatically evaluated targets, prioritizing them by threat, and then tracked them, but it did allow for manual intervention. The system could also accept plots from other systems and units. During the 1970s and 1980s different ADAWS systems were introduced, depending on the weapons fit of vessels. The ADAWS systems on the Type 42s were modernized throughout these ships' careers, not least with the addition of the Captain's Combat Aid in the late 1990s, which provided summaries of weapon status, target data and target priorities to a ship's captain on a single console. The Type 45's tactical command system was a quantum leap from the ADAWS systems, which still had at their core 1970s technology; the CMS-1 is a distributed system linked by an Ethernet data transfer network to weapons and sensors. CMS-1 provides a full tactical picture, evaluates threats, assigns weapon systems and undertakes kill assessments. It is said to be able to track over one hundred targets and deal with at least ten separate immediate threats.

The operations room of HMS *Daring* in 2009: the CMS-1 command system uses at least 25 multi-function consoles, each with three digital screens per operator. (MoD/Open Government Licence v3.0)

System	Fitted on
ADAWS 1	County-class Batch 2
ADAWS 2	Type 82
ADAWS 4	Batch 1 Type 42
ADAWS 7	Batch 2 Type 42
ADAWS 8	Batch 3 Type 42, later Batch 2 Type 42
CMS-1	Type 45

Communications	System	Description
Satellite communications	SCOT	Fitted on Batch 2 Counties and Type 42s from the late 1970s onwards for communication with the Skynet satellite system.
	OE-82	US satellite communication system. Fitted to Type 82 in the late 1980s.
	INMARSAT	Maritime satellite navigation system
Tactical data links	Link 11	NATO standard system allowing tactical data transfers among ships. Fitted to Type 82 and Type 42 from 1980.
	Link 10	A cheaper version of Link 11 fitted to Counties, Type 82 and Type 42 by the Falklands.
	Link 14	Teleprinter datalink for non-Link 11 ships
	Link 16	A complementary system to Link 11 with greater capacity delivering data in pulses. On Type 42s by the mid-1990s. Fitted to Type 45s.
	Link 22	Complement to Links 11 and 16. Fitted on Type 45.
Underwater telephones	Type 185	Allows ships to communicate with submarines.
	Type 2008	

Communications among ships, with other units and with land-based stations have become increasingly important for modern naval warfare as a tactical picture is invariably built up from many sources, creating a network of systems and platforms. Some naval communication systems used on British destroyers are summarized in the table above.

COUNTY-CLASS DESTROYERS

Design development

From the late 1940s the Admiralty investigated ways in which to get anti-aircraft guided missiles to sea, with the British-developed Sea Slug as the main weapon system under consideration. At the very earliest stages in 1947 it was planned to install Sea Slug in existing or planned cruiser designs. However, by the late 1940s and early 1950s, the navy's strategic priority was now convoy defence in a possible second Battle of the Atlantic against Soviet

Ships from a number of NATO members in Malta harbour while participating in exercises. This photograph was taken in 1961, the year before the first County class entered service. Many of the ships in service with NATO navies, 16 years after the end of World War II, were still of that vintage. (Imperial War Museum, HU 102648)

submarines. As a result, much design effort went into developing coastal and ocean escorts armed with Sea Slug-guided missiles, alongside fleet task force missile escorts. The Sea Slug system was bulky, so these would not have been small vessels. The landing craft maintenance ship HMS *Girdle Ness* was converted as a trials ship for the Sea Slug system between 1953 and 1956 and for a time it was thought that she might act as a prototype for the coastal missile escort, but she did not have the capacity for a wartime complement. By 1955, and following a change in naval strategy focusing on cold war and warm war 'East of Suez' task-force operations rather than convoy defence, the projected missile escorts coalesced around two designs that were not pure missile ships. The first was a missile cruiser with the traditional 6-inch gun armament of the cruiser forward and a Sea Slug launcher aft. The second was a missile destroyer in a similar configuration with 4.5-inch destroyer mountings forward and Sea Slug aft. The missile cruiser, which had grown to over 18,000 tons in its final version, was cancelled in January 1957. Only the missile destroyer design now remained; it had originated as a way to combine a minimum fleet missile escort proposed in November 1954 with a then-planned conventional destroyer design. With the cancellation of the missile cruiser, the design began to grow in size and capability, and also take on some of the 'cruiser' characteristics of the cancelled larger vessel.

By September 1956 the missile destroyer design was armed with two twin 4.5-inch guns in Mk VI mountings, a Sea Slug launcher with 18 missiles, eight anti-submarine torpedo tubes, the Mark X 'Limbo' anti-submarine mortar, and two twin 40mm guns. Propulsion was via a combination of gas turbines and steam turbines: the latter providing the main machinery with the former providing a boost capacity allowing for accelerations in speed at short notice. At various stages over the next two years changes were made to

HMS *London* in 1980 just before she was decommissioned. The Batch 1 Counties could be distinguished from their later sisters owing to their Type 965 AKE I air-search radar on the mainmast: the AKE I had only one 'bedstead' rectangular array rather than two. (Hugh Llewelyn/CC BY-SA 2.0)

the design: the 40mm guns were replaced by two Sea Cat short-range anti-aircraft missile launchers, the Sea Slug missile stowage was increased to 24, and eventually the Limbo mortar and torpedo tubes were replaced by a flight deck for a light helicopter and eventually a hangar and facilities for a large Wessex anti-submarine helicopter. This last-minute addition of a helicopter hangar was only possible by placing the hangar forward of the large Type 901 Sea Slug guidance radar and between the two Sea Cat launchers, which meant for an awkward process to get the helicopter out of its hangar and onto the flight deck.

In addition, a number of changes gave the design a 'cruiser' feel: space for an Admiral and his staff, including an Admiral's bridge, and even a partial traditional wooden deck forward to aid in 'showing-the-flag' duties. It was certainly a very powerful and impressive-looking ship design, the size and lines of which evoked both the old cruisers of a previous generation and the high-technology capability of the guided missile era.

HMS *Hampshire*, 1963	
Displacement (tons)	5,440 standard, 6,200 full-load
Dimensions (ft in: length/beam/draught)	521ft/54ft/20ft 6in
Armament	4 4.5-inch Mk 6s; Sea Slug Mk 1; 2 Sea Cats; 2 40mm; 1 Wessex
Sensors	Radar: Types 965 (AKE I), 992, 277Q, 978, 903, 901, 262
	Sonar: Types 177, 162M
Machinery	Combined Steam and Gas ('COSAG') 2 steam turbines/boilers, 4 G6 gas turbines
	30 knots
	Range: 3,500 nautical miles at 28 knots
Complement	470

Construction programme

The design had been approved by the Admiralty Board in March 1957, even though a number of changes would be made after this date, and the first of

THE COUNTY CLASS

This plate shows HMS *Antrim* in 1977. The high freeboard of the County class, which helped give these ships their elegant appearance, was largely the result of the stowage and assembly requirements for the Sea Slug missile system. Missiles were stored horizontally above the waterline, and had their fins attached as they progressed along the below-decks assembly area on a track and trolley system, before appearing through hatches onto the launcher aft. The plan also shows the awkward hangar arrangements for the Wessex helicopter. A late addition to the design, the large Type 901 tracker radar could not be moved, so the hangar was placed forward of the radar, with the hangar door to one side and the Wessex being manoeuvred past the Sea Cat launcher to reach the flight deck. From forward to aft, HMS *Antrim* has a twin 4.5-inch Mk 6 mounting, launchers for four Exocet missiles (which had recently replaced the second twin 4.5-inch mounting), and atop the bridge structure is the Type 903 gunnery fire-control radar. The foremast has the Type 992Q surface-search radar at the top with the Type 978 navigation radar halfway up. Either side of the foremast are 20mm light-gun mountings. Abreast the first funnel are Corvus chaff launchers. Atop the mainmast is the large Type 965 AKE II radar (known informally as the 'double bedstead') with the Type 278 height finder immediately below it facing aft. Either side of the second funnel are the Type 904 director radars for the Sea Cat launchers, which can be seen either side of the hangar. Behind the hangar is the large Type 901 Sea Slug tracker radar, and aft of the flight deck is the twin Sea Slug launcher.

class was laid down in 1959, having been ordered under the 1955–56 estimates, alongside a sister vessel. These ships, named *Hampshire* and *Devonshire*, resurrected the county names of inter-war-built heavy cruisers, which had had gallant World War II careers, and were followed by two more vessels under the 1956–57 estimates, named *Kent* and *London*. Despite their size, complexity and the last-minute nature of many of the changes, the ships were built at commendable speed with the entire first batch being completed by the end of 1963.

County Class, Batch 1

Pendant	Name	Yard	Laid down	Launched	Completed
D06	*Hampshire*	John Brown, Clydebank	26/03/59	16/03/61	15/03/63
D02	*Devonshire*	Cammell Laird, Birkenhead	09/03/59	10/06/60	15/11/62
D12	*Kent*	Harland and Wolff, Belfast	01/03/60	27/09/61	15/08/63
D16	*London*	Swan Hunter, Wallsend	26/02/60	07/12/61	14/11/63

After the ordering of the first group of ships, attention turned to the next batch. Radical plans for a wholly new class of even larger vessels were considered but dropped, and the next batch included an updated suite of radar and sonar and the Mark 2 version of Sea Slug. It had been planned to build six in the second batch, but the last four were cancelled in expectation of orders for a Sea Slug-armed helicopter cruiser. When it became clear that the helicopter cruiser would not be built the last two Counties, *Antrim* and *Norfolk*, were ordered.

HMS *Antrim*, 1975

Displacement (tons)	5,440 standard, 6,200 full-load
Dimensions (ft in: length/beam/draught)	522ft/53ft/20ft
Armament	2 4.5-inch Mk 6s; 4 Exocets; Sea Slug Mk 2 (39 missiles); 2 Sea Cats; 2 20mm guns; 1 Wessex
Sensors	Radar: Types 965 (AKE II), 992Q, 278, 978, 992R, 904, 903, 901
	Sonar: Types 184M, 162M
Command system	ADAWS 1
Machinery	COSAG propulsion: 2 steam turbines/boilers, 4 G6 gas turbines
	30 knots
	Range: 3,500 nautical miles at 28 knots
Complement	470

County Class, Batch 2

Pendant	Name	Yard	Laid down	Launched	Completed
D19	*Glamorgan*	Vickers Armstrong, Newcastle upon Tyne	13/09/62	09/07/64	13/10/66
D20	*Fife*	Fairfield, Govan	31/05/62	09/07/64	21/06/66
D18	*Antrim*	Fairfield, Govan	20/01/66	19/10/67	14/07/70
D21	*Norfolk*	Swan Hunter, Wallsend, Tyne and Wear	15/03/66	16/11/67	07/03/70

In-service modifications

The Batch 1 ships received few changes to their basic equipment over their service lives; however, their Type 992 radar was replaced by the Type 992Q

and their Sea Cat system was updated to GWS 22 standard. Plans to upgrade them to Batch 2 standards were considered and dropped in the late 1960s. The Batch 2 ships did, however, receive a number of significant changes to their equipment. In 1973 *Norfolk* was fitted with Exocet anti-ship missile canisters in place of a second 4.5-inch mounting, and, following trials of the system in 1974, they were fitted to the other Batch 2 ships over the next three years. Following the Falklands conflict *Fife* was refitted with additional light guns, STWS 1 torpedo tubes and Lynx in place of the Wessex. *Glamorgan*'s refit entailed the removal of the Sea Cat launchers and their replacement by 40mm guns, an indication that these vessels were no longer regarded as front-line ships. The Counties were elegant and imposing ships, but they suffered from their heavy manpower requirements and the rapid obsolescence of the Sea Slug system around which they were designed. As a result, their careers were relatively short in Royal Navy service, although the Batch 2 ships lasted for a number of years in Chilean service.

HMS *Fife* in her original configuration before the addition of Exocets. The Batch 2 Counties had the Type 965 AKE II radar with its 'double bedstead' of two rectangular arrays, one above the other. (MoD Naval Historical Branch)

TYPE 82 DESTROYER: HMS *BRISTOL*

Design development

In the early 1960s development began on a lightweight successor to Sea Slug. Initial plans showed a system installed on a vessel the size of a Leander-class frigate (around 2,500 tons displacement) with much of its aft armament (Sea Cat, Wasp helicopter, Limbo anti-submarine mortar) removed and replaced by a twin-armed launcher. This initial frigate ancestry explains the use of a 'frigate'-Type number designation, with the eighty range in 82 denoting a

HMS *Bristol* firing a Sea Dart missile. As the first ship fitted with Sea Dart, she underwent a long period of trials of the system in her first years after completion. (Imperial War Museum, MH 27568)

general-purpose vessel. As the design developed, its capability increased and so did its design and cost. The forward medium gun was replaced by the Australian Ikara anti-submarine torpedo delivery missile system. This necessitated a significant increase in tactical command capacity to deal with both air defence and anti-submarine threats with two very complex systems. A decision was made to install the mixed gas and steam propulsion of the County class – which gave a commendable short-notice 'sprint' capability – but increased the size, cost and crew of this design quite considerably. In addition, the medium gun was reinstated in the design, which also increased the size of the ship. Finally, as it became clear that the Type 82 would be the definitive successor to the Counties, and that she would be the main air-defence escort of the projected CVA01 carriers, she was fitted with the command facilities of the Counties and the huge Dutch Type 966 'broomstick'

B

THE TYPE 82

This plate shows HMS *Bristol* as built in 1973. Like the County-class destroyers, *Bristol* had Combined Steam and Gas turbine propulsion (COSAG), which meant that in addition to a steam turbine room and boiler room, the uptakes of which came through the first funnel, she had a gas turbine room aft of the steam turbines that housed the four G6 gas turbines. The uptakes for these emerged in two parallel funnels behind the main mast. This meant that *Bristol* was the first major British warship since the large Abdiel-class cruiser minelayers of World War II to have three funnels. From forward to aft, *Bristol* has a single 4.5-inch gun in a Mk 8 automatic mounting; behind that is the well for the Ikara anti-submarine missile system covered to protect the launcher from the elements. Next can be seen the radome for the forward Type 909 tracker radar. Either side of the bridge are two Ikara tracker radars and above the bridge is the small Type 978 navigation radar. The short mainmast includes the Type 965 AKE II air-search radar and either side of the first funnel are 20mm light weapons. The tall mainmast is topped with the Type 992Q radar and behind the rear funnels is the radome of the aft Type 909 tracker. Behind this is the twin-armed Sea Dart launcher and then the flight deck for a Wasp or Lynx helicopter (although there was no hangar for such an aircraft).

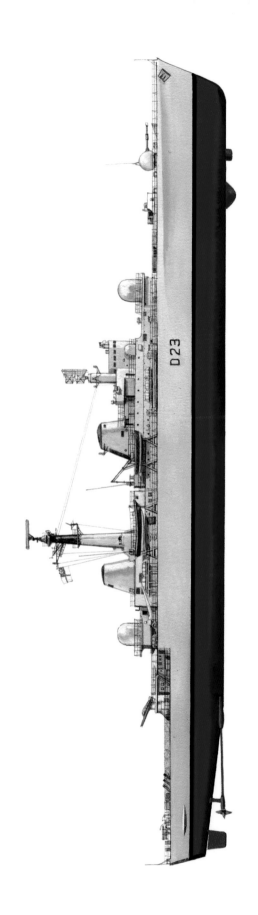

long-range search radar. At the end of the design process, the Type 82 had tripled in size and cost. With the cancellation of the CVA01 carrier in the 1966 Defence Review, the Type 82 seemed to be an expensive anachronism. The Sea Lords fought hard to have one vessel of the design built, partly to salvage something from the wreckage of the old shipbuilding programme, and partly to get at least one Sea Dart system to sea as soon as possible. In the event, delays in the building of HMS *Bristol* meant that she was completed less than two years before the first ship of the new Type 42 design.

An image of HMS *Bristol*, taken in November 1982 on return from the South Atlantic, showing the aft half of the ship to good effect. The top halves of her masts and her funnel cowls had been painted grey on the way south. (Barry Skeates/CC BY-SA 2.0)

HMS *Bristol* in 2012 as a static cadet-training ship in Portsmouth harbour. Her weapons, sensors and tops of her masts have been removed, but she is still a commissioned naval vessel. She took on this new role in 1993 after serving as the Dartmouth training ship from 1987 to 1991. (Hugh Llewelyn/CC BY-SA 2.0)

HMS *Bristol*, 1973	
Displacement (tons)	6,100 standard, 7,100 full-load
Dimensions (ft in: length/beam/draught)	507ft/55ft/24ft 7in
Armament	1 4.5-inch Mk 8; Sea Dart (40 missiles); Ikara; Limbo
Sensors	Radar: Types 965 (AKE II), 992Q, 909, 978
	Sonar: Type 184M, 170, 162M
Command system	ADAWS 2
Machinery	COSAG: 2 steam turbines/boilers, 2 Olympus gas turbines
	30 knots
	Range: 5,000 nautical miles at 18 knots
Complement	433

Construction programme

It had been envisaged that either six or four Type 82s would be built, but all except the first ship of the class were cancelled in the 1966 defence review. Like the County class before it, the Type 82 revived an old cruiser name. In the case of *Bristol*, this was a light cruiser of 1910. *Bristol* was finally completed with the less capable Type 965 AKE II in place of the Type 988.

Type 82					
Pendant	Name	Yard	Laid down	Launched	Completed
D23	*Bristol*	Swan Hunter, Tyne and Wear	15/11/67	30/06/69	31/03/73

In-service modifications

In the late 1970s *Bristol* received the Link 11 and SCOT communication systems. After the Falklands she received additional light weapons, and in refit between 1984 and 1986 she received the Type 1022 search radar in place of the Type 965, but her Ikara system and Limbo mortar were removed. *Bristol* was a one off: a carrier escort without an aircraft carrier, and a large warship requiring a large crew but which also seemed under-armed, particularly after the Ikara was removed. In these circumstances it is not surprising that her active service ended in 1991.

TYPE 42 DESTROYERS: SHEFFIELD CLASS

Design development

The cancellation of the new aircraft carrier, and of its air-defence escort (barring one vessel, HMS *Bristol*), created an urgent need for a new design to carry Sea Dart. The Sea Slug system of the Counties was facing obsolescence, so Sea Dart ships were needed quickly. Design studies under the Future Fleet Working Party worked up a series of Sea Dart destroyers from the absolute minimum of a vessel armed with Sea Dart and almost nothing else, to a capable Sea Dart destroyer of 4,400 tons. The working party recommended this last vessel, but this and many of its other proposals were rejected by the Sea Lords who were mindful of the vulnerability of the navy after the cancellation of the carrier – the Secretary of State for Defence, Denis Healey, was not at the time keen to approve large new warships – and the Treasury was adamant that cheaper vessels be procured. As a result, the working party's design options were reconsidered and the design one step above the minimum (with Sea Dart, but also with space for

HMS *Sheffield* as built. Note the 'elephant ears' on the funnel. She and the Argentine *Hércules* were the only Type 42s completed with this feature. Note also the lack of torpedo tubes, SCOT satellite radomes and the lack of intercepts on the mainmast. (MoD Naval Historical Branch)

This cutaway plate shows HMS *Glasgow* as built. She incorporated many of the additions that had been introduced incrementally in the Batch 1 ships of the class. She had a Lynx HAS2 helicopter rather than a Wasp, she was fitted with STWS 1 torpedo tubes and she had UAA-1 intercepts just below the Type 992Q radar on the mainmast. The cutaway shows the propulsion of the Type 42s. They were the first class of major western warship which was designed with all-gas turbine propulsion. Marine gas turbines are jet engines which are powered by mixing fuel and air into a gas and then compressing that gas to cause combustion, which then drives the turbines. The Counties and Type 82s had a mixture of traditional steam propulsion and gas turbines. Instead, the Type 42s had two Olympus gas turbines for speed, and two Tyne gas turbines for economical cruising at up to 18 knots. Four diesel generators forward and aft of these turbines provided the non-propulsion power for the ship. These are shown here as well as the gearboxes which transferred power to and from the Olympus and the Tyne. Also shown in the cutaway are the workings of the 4.5-inch Mk 8 mounting and the Sea Dart system. On commissioning, HMS *Glasgow* was made half leader of 7th Destroyer Squadron. She would have had a thin black stripe near the top of the funnel and number seven painted on each side of the funnel.

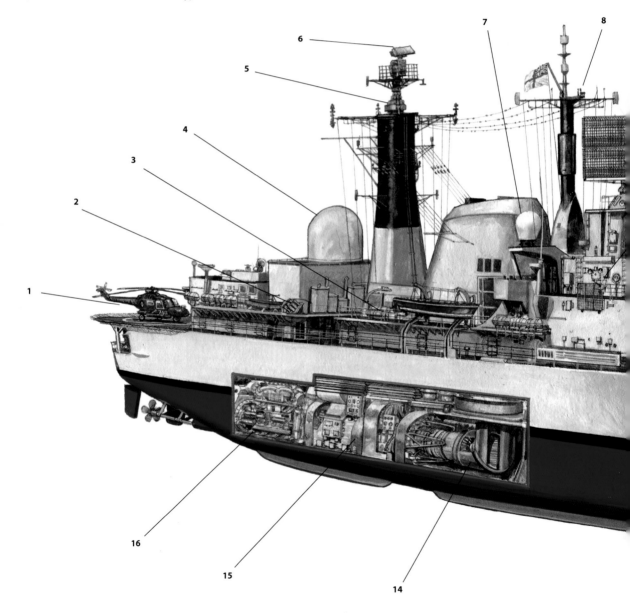

1. Lynx HAS2 helicopter
2. Corvus chaff launcher
3. STWS 1 torpedo tubes
4. Aft Type 909 tracker/illuminator radar
5. UAA-1 intercept
6. Type 992Q target indication/surveillance radar
7. SCOT satellite communication aerial
8. Type 1006 navigation radar
9. Type 965 AKE II air search radar
10. 20mm gun
11. Forward Type 909 tracker/illuminator radar
12. Sea Dart launcher
13. 4.5-inch Mk 8 gun
14. Olympus gas turbines
15. Tyne gas turbines
16. Aft diesel generators

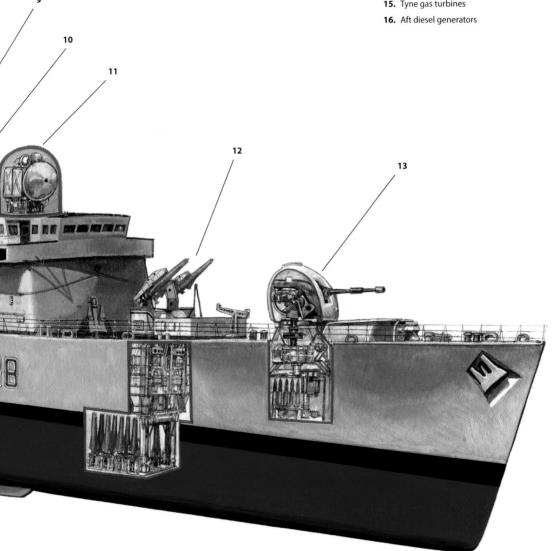

a torpedo-armed helicopter and its hangar) was accepted for further development. This vessel became the Type 42 destroyer. The design was developed at some speed, and incorporated a slightly scaled-down Sea Dart system. During design development the capability of the Sea Dart system was augmented: the original single-arm launcher was replaced by a light twin-arm launcher when it became clear it could be fitted, and a second Type 909 tracker/illuminator radar was added aft to allow the guidance of two missiles in flight. The resulting vessel was impressive in that it carried a considerable range of capabilities on a relatively small hull. In retrospect, perhaps the greatest weakness was the small 22-missile magazine in all vessels of the class. However, in the context of 1967, before the Soviets had introduced the next generation of bombers, and a residual 'East of Suez' capability was expected, the relatively small size of the missile magazine is at least partly understandable.

HMS *Sheffield*, 1975

Displacement (tons)	3,500 standard, 4,100 full-load
Dimensions (ft in: length/beam/draught)	410ft/47ft/19ft
Armament	1 4.5-inch Mk 8; 2 20mm; Sea Dart (22 missiles); Wasp
Sensors	Radar: Types 965 (AKE II), 992Q, 909, 1006
	Sonar: Types 184M, 162M
Command system	ADAWS 4
Machinery	Combined Gas or Gas ('COGOG'): 2 Olympus, 2 Tyne gas turbines
	30 knots
	Range: 4,100 nautical miles at 18 knots
Complement	253

Two Type 42 destroyers were ordered by the Argentinian government in 1970. The first, ARA *Hércules*, was built at Vickers in Barrow, the second, ARA *Santisima Trinidad*, in Argentina. They were completed in 1976 and 1981 respectively, the latter delayed following the explosion of a bomb planted by a far-left group inside the vessel during building.

Construction programme

The first of the class, HMS *Sheffield*, was ordered on 14 November 1968. Orders then followed regularly until 1979 (when the last three of the class were ordered in the space of one month). The first six vessels formed Batch 1 of the class, all being completed to the same design. *Sheffield* was completed without STWS 1 torpedo tubes for Mk 44 or Mk 46 torpedoes, while both *Sheffield* and *Birmingham* had a Wasp helicopter on board until the Lynx was available.

Type 42, Batch 1

Pendant	Name	Yard	Laid down	Launched	Completed
D80	*Sheffield*	Vickers, Barrow-in-Furness	15/01/70	10/06/71	16/02/75
D86	*Birmingham*	Cammell Laird, Birkenhead	28/03/72	30/07/73	03/12/76
D108	*Cardiff*	Vickers, Barrow-in-Furness; Swan Hunter, Hebburn, Tyne and Wear	03/11/72	22/02/74	24/09/79
D118	*Coventry*	Cammell Laird, Birkenhead	29/01/73	21/06/74	20/10/78
D87	*Newcastle*	Swan Hunter, Neptune Yard, Tyne and Wear	21/02/73	24/04/75	23/03/78
D88	*Glasgow*	Swan Hunter, Neptune Yard, Tyne and Wear	07/03/74	14/04/76	24/05/79

The Batch 2 ships contained a number of modifications to the Batch 1 design: a modified version of the ADAWS tactical command system was installed (ADAWS 7), the Type 1022 long-range air-search radar replaced the now obsolescent Type 965, and the ship's flight deck was squared off rather than rounded as in the first batch.

HMS *Exeter* as built. Note the blue hull below the waterline. This self-polishing anti-fouling paint was tested on *Exeter* at an experimental stage when it was only available in this colour. The trials were a success and the paint (now no longer blue) was applied to the hulls of the rest of the fleet. (MoD Naval Historical Branch)

HMS *Exeter*, 1981

Displacement (tons)	3,500 standard, 4,100 full-load
Dimensions (ft in: length/beam/draught)	410ft/47ft/19ft
Armament	1 4.5-inch Mk 8; 2 20mm; Sea Dart (22 missiles); STWS 1, Lynx
Sensors	Radar: Types 1022, 992R, 909, 1006
	Sonar: Types 184M, 162M
Command system	ADAWS 7
Machinery	COGOG: 2 Olympus / 2 Tyne gas turbines
	30 knots
	Range: 4,100 nautical miles at 18 knots
Complement	253

Type 42, Batch 2

Pendant	Name	Yard	Laid down	Launched	In service
D89	*Exeter*	Swan Hunter, Wallsend, Tyne and Wear	22/07/76	25/04/78	19/09/80
D90	*Southampton*	Vosper Thornycroft, Woolston, Southampton	21/10/76	29/01/79	23/07/81
D91	*Nottingham*	Vosper Thornycroft, Woolston, Southampton	06/02/78	12/02/80	08/04/83
D92	*Liverpool*	Cammell Laird, Birkenhead	05/07/78	25/09/80	09/07/82

The next, and final, batch of vessels was lengthened by 52 feet to improve seaworthiness (the first two batches were notoriously 'wet' forward in heavy seas), endurance and habitability. An increase in the size of the Sea Dart magazine was considered but rejected due to the expense and difficulty of redesigning the magazine drum and hoists upwards to the launchers. Two further Batch 3 vessels were in the projected naval programme in 1979 and 1980, but they were cancelled in the cuts leading up to the 1981 Defence Review.

HMS *Manchester*, the first of the Batch 3 Type 42s, as completed in 1982. She has not yet had the additional light weapons added, reflecting her Falklands experience, but the image clearly shows the longer and more elegant lines of the last four ships of the class. (MoD Naval Historical Branch)

HMS *Edinburgh*, 1985	
Displacement (tons)	4,000 standard, 4,800 full-load
Dimensions (ft in: length/beam/draught)	463ft/50ft/19ft
Armament	1 4.5-inch Mk 8; 2 30mm, 4 20mm; Sea Dart (22 missiles); Lynx
Sensors	Radar: Types 1022, 992R, 909, 1006
	Sonar: Types 2016, 162M
Command system	ADAWS 8
Machinery	COGOG propulsion: 2 Olympus / 2 Tyne gas turbines
	30 knots
	Range: 4,100 nautical miles at 18 knots
Complement	253

Type 42, Batch 3					
Pendant	Name	Yard	Laid down	Launched	Completed
D95	*Manchester*	Vickers, Barrow-in-Furness	19/05/79	24/11/80	16/12/82
D96	*Gloucester*	Vosper Thornycroft, Woolston, Southampton	26/10/79	02/11/82	11/09/85
D97	*Edinburgh*	Cammell Laird, Birkenhead	08/09/80	14/04/83	18/12/85
D98	*York*	Swan Hunter, Wallsend, Tyne and Wear	18/01/80	21/06/82	09/08/85

In-service modifications

The experience of the Falklands conflict resulted in the addition of further light weapons to all surviving ships in the class. All Batch 1 vessels were updated to Batch 2 standards by the late 1980s with the Type 965 radar being replaced by the Type 1022 and the ADAWS 4 command system being replaced by ADAWS 7. By 1989 further improvements to the ships' self-defence capability were made with the addition of two Vulcan Phalanx close-in weapon systems, either side of the ships' funnel. Plans to install a lightweight version of the Sea Wolf missile system on Batch 3 ships (involving the reduction

TYPE 42, BATCHES 2 AND 3

1: HMS *Exeter*

The Type 42 Batch 2 included a number of improvements to the Batch 1 design. Most notable was the replacement of the Type 965 radar with the Type 1022, which was more effective at detecting low-flying targets. Most of the improvements were either not externally visible or barely so: the NATO standard Link 11 communications system was fitted, the Type 992R radar replaced the Type 992Q on the mainmast and other improvements were made to the communications capability. This plate shows HMS *Exeter* in 2007 towards the end of her career. As a result of the Falklands War, two Vulcan Phalanx close-in weapon systems had been placed amidships either side of the funnel. These rapid-firing guns included their own integral radar housed in a radome above the gun. In addition, the Type 992R had been replaced by the Type 996 on the mainmast, new navigating radars had been added, the Lynx helicopter updated to HMA8 standards, and the electronic warfare capabilities modernized. To compensate for the increased top-weight of this additional equipment, the STWS torpedo tubes had been landed.

2: HMS *Edinburgh*

The Type 42 Batch 3 ships were lengthened by 65 feet and their beam broadened. This plate shows HMS *Edinburgh* as completed in 1985. She was completed with the first stage of the post-Falklands light weapons enhancement with two Oerlikon/BMARC 30mm mountings abreast the funnel and two 20mm mountings abreast the rear of the hangar. Her other improvements over the Batch 2 ships were STWS 2 torpedo tubes (which can be seen here on a platform below the mainmast) which could fire the Stingray torpedo, and the Sea Gnat decoy system in place of Corvus. The stretched hull made the Batch 3 ships much less 'wet' forward in heavy seas, but it turned out that the hull was as a result weaker than planned; in the 1990s the Batch 3 ships were given reinforcing strakes at the top of the hull.

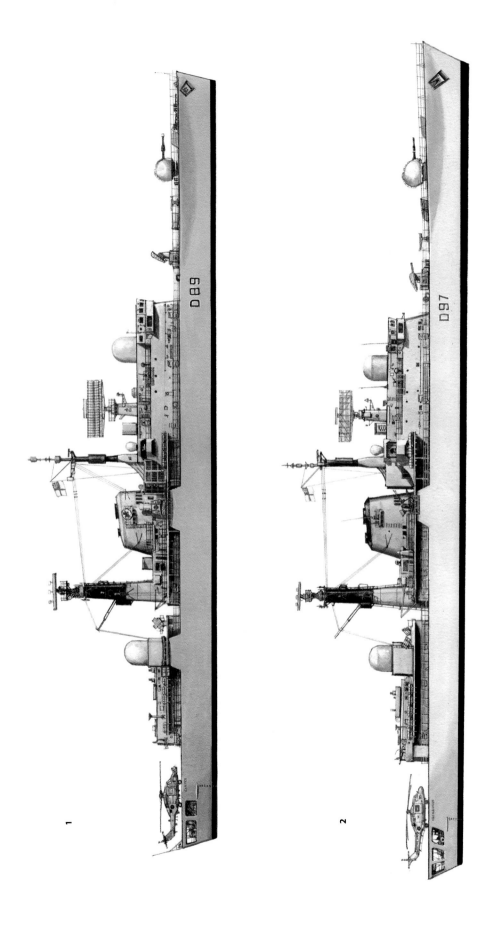

1

2

HMS *Manchester* looking aft as built. Note the square stern of the ship in comparison with the rounded stern of the Batch 1 vessels. (MoD Naval Historical Branch)

to one Phalanx – which would be placed forward between the 4.5-inch gun and the Sea Dart launcher – and the placing of Sea Wolf launchers abeam the funnel) were cancelled in the 1990 Defence Review. HMS *Edinburgh* had already been fitted for, but not with, the Sea Wolf, when this cancellation occurred: her Phalanx being moved forward and bow bulwarks heightened to shelter the Phalanx from spray. During the early 1990s further modifications were made to the vessels. The table below shows HMS *Liverpool* in the mid-1990s. By this time all the surviving ships of this class had been modernized to these standards including significant updates to the Sea Dart system. Note that the STWS torpedo tubes have been removed because of top-weight issues deriving from the increased electronic fit.

HMS *Liverpool*, 1994	
Displacement (tons)	3,500 standard, 4,250 full-load
Dimensions (ft in: length/beam/draught)	410ft/47ft/19ft
Armament	1 4.5-inch Mk 8; 4 20mm; 2 Phalanx CIWS; Sea Dart Mod 2 (22 missiles); Lynx
Sensors	Radar: Types 1022, 996, 909 (1), 1006
	Sonar: Types 2050, 162M
Command system	ADAWS 7
Machinery	COGOG: 2 Olympus / 2 Tyne gas turbines
	28 knots
	Range: 4,100 nautical miles at 18 knots
Complement	299

By the late 2000s the surviving ships had seen further modifications, including the replacement of the Type 1006 navigation radar with the Type 1007 and the Type 1008, an updated version of the Phalanx, and modernization of the ADAWS system in some ships. Most distinctively the Batch 3 ships in the class had the fibreglass dome of the 4.5-inch mounting replaced with a multi-faced dome with improved radar signal reduction capabilities. During the ships' service a whole range of updates were also made to the ships' communications systems, electronic countermeasures and other electronic warfare systems.

HMS *Glasgow* on Exercise *Distant Drum* in 1983. She has recently emerged from refit and repairs, following the Falklands conflict, with new positions amidships and abreast the hangar for additional light weapons, although these have not yet been fitted. (mashleymorgan/CC BY-SA 2.0)

HMS *Edinburgh* in her final form: the raised bulwarks at her bow were a unique feature of this ship and a legacy of a cancelled attempt to place the Sea Wolf missile system on these ships. (MoD/Open Government Licence v3.0)

The Type 42s were the mainstay of the Royal Navy's shipborne air defence from the 1980s through to the end of the 2000s. They ensured that as many Sea Dart systems were put to sea as possible, although most of the ships only appeared in service at a time when they would have been vulnerable to Soviet saturation air attacks. Sea Dart was much updated and improved throughout its life, but by the mid-2000s it was obsolescent.

TYPE 45 DESTROYERS: DARING CLASS

Design development
Successors to the Type 42 began to be considered even before the first ship of the class had been completed. The Type 43 design was a very large destroyer

HMS *Defender*. The superstructure shape of the Type 45s owes a certain amount to the Horizon design of the 1990s. (MoD/Open Government Licence v3.0)

armed with two separate Sea Dart systems, and a large Sea King helicopter, the flight deck of which was in the centre of the ship between the first and second funnels. It was planned that when the Type 42 programme finished, construction would immediately resume on the new Type 43. However, defence economies in 1980 caused this design to be shrunk in size and capability, and then cancelled. The Type 44 design then took its place. This in turn was cancelled in the 1981 Defence Review.

	Type 43 (1978)	Type 44 (May 1980)
Displacement (tons)	6,000 standard	5,500 tonnes deep load
Dimensions	557ft length, 58ft beam	459ft length
Armament	1 4.5-inch Mk 8; 2 GWS31 Sea Dart (2 twin launchers); 4 lightweight Sea Wolf launchers; 4 Exocets; 1 Sea King helicopter	1 Oto Melara 76mm; GWS31 Sea Dart (twin launcher, 32 missiles); 4 lightweight Sea Wolf launchers (60 missiles); Ikara (33 missiles); anti-ship missile system
Sensors	Radar: Types 1022, 967/968, 2 1006, 4 909, 2 910 Sonar: Type 2016	Radar: Types 1030, 967/968, 2 909M, 2 910M Sonar: Type 2016
Command system	ADAWS 9	CACS 3
Machinery	COGOG; 4 SM1A gas turbines Range: 5,900 nautical miles at 18.5 knots	–
Complement	303	303

 TYPE 45

This plate shows HMS *Daring* as completed. From forward to aft, the 4.5-inch gun (recycled from a decommissioned Type 42 destroyer but with a new radar signal-reducing housing) is followed by the deckhouse for the 48 Sylver vertical launch canisters for Aster missiles. Between this deckhouse and the bridge is space for Harpoon anti-ship missiles, although these have not yet been fitted to most of the class, and above and behind the bridge is the large sloped foremast with the rotating Sampson radar at the top. The foremast also holds the satellite communication equipment, various electronic warfare arrays and the Type 1048 surface-search radar. Either side and just forward of the fore funnel are sponsons for two 30mm mountings; aft of these are the two Vulcan Phalanx close-in weapon systems. The mainmast holds the long-range S1850M air-search radar, and immediately aft is the short aft funnel, its exhaust at an angle to avoid the search-radar array. Either side of the hangar are covered recesses, which reduce radar signature, for the ship's boats. The hangar is large enough for either one Merlin anti-submarine helicopter or two Lynx helicopters (soon to be replaced by the Lynx Wildcat). Shown here is the single Lynx currently carried by ships of the class. The flight deck has sufficient space to land a Chinook helicopter, making it roughly four times the area of the Type 42 flight deck.

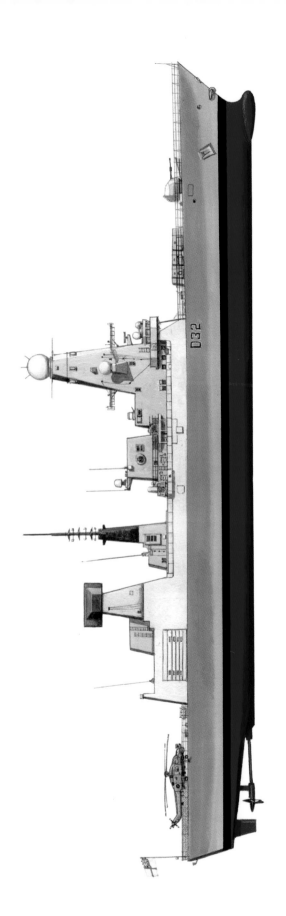
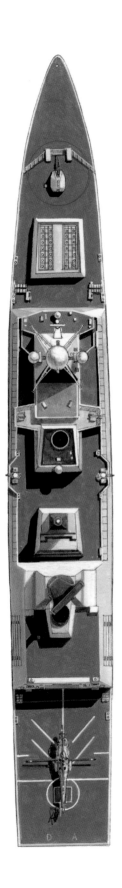

The first Type 45s shipped Lynx helicopters. This image shows the first landing of a larger helicopter – in this case a large Sea King – on the flight deck of a Type 45. This gives an indication of the huge size of the Type 45 flight deck in comparison to that of the Counties and Type 42. (MoD/Open Government Licence v3.0)

HMS *Duncan* seen from above in Cardiff docks for the 2014 NATO summit. This view shows the deck layout of the Type 45. Note the racks of Harpoon between the bridge and the Sylver launchers. There is understood to be space for 12 additional missile launchers between the current Sylvers and the 4.5-inch gun. (MoD/Open Government Licence v3.0)

The 1981 Defence Review's initial outcomes suggested that the air-defence destroyer would be phased out of the Royal Navy by the early 1990s, with the last Type 42s being removed from service more than ten years early and no replacements being built. As the review progressed however, this decision was reversed but no long-term replacement for the Type 42 was in development following the cancellation of the Type 44.

The Falklands War transformed the future of air-defence destroyers by definitively demonstrating their utility, and the (partial) effectiveness of the Sea Dart system. By 1983 the British had joined the NATO frigate replacement programme (NFR90), a multilateral programme across NATO to produce the next-generation medium-sized warship. The Royal Navy's commitment was to the area air-defence version of the design. The NFR90 stayed in development throughout the 1980s without any orders being placed, and following the end of the Cold War the programme collapsed as defence cuts and different priorities caused the participating states to follow divergent routes. It appears that some design work took place on a national British basis for a while after the cancellation of the NFR90 (one defence annual describing a 'Type 84 frigate' of over 6,000 tons), but by 1993 the British had joined with the French and Italians to develop the trilateral Horizon air-defence frigate. The British stayed within the programme until 1997, but differences in priorities and requirements, not least that the Royal Navy required a full area-defence capability (requiring the Sampson radar and Astor 30 long-range missiles), meant cooperation was no longer seen to be worthwhile. In 1998 design work started on a national alternative inheriting many elements of the Horizon programme, not least the Aster missile family and the Sylver vertical launch system.

In addition to the formidable Astor/Sylver/Sampson combination, the Type 45, partly to save costs, inherited some weapon systems from the preceding class: Mk 8 4.5-inch guns were transferred from decommissioned Type 42s, while some elements of capability were 'fitted for – but not with' such as Harpoon anti-ship missiles and anti-submarine torpedoes. At one stage it was planned to complete the class without any sonar capability at all. Plans to fit the US Collaborative Engagement Capability system, which would allow for the creation of a single real-time tactical picture across ships carrying the system, was deferred in 2012. As of 2015 only two in the class, *Duncan* and *Diamond*, have been fitted with Harpoon. The propulsion of the class is also a revolutionary leap from previous destroyers. Two gas turbines and two diesels power, through electric transmission, both the ship's systems and the ship's propulsion. Previously, separate systems had powered and driven British warships.

HMS *Daring*, 2009	
Displacement (tons)	5,800 standard, 7,350 full-load
Dimensions (ft in: length/beam/draught)	500ft/69ft/24ft
Armament	1 4.5-inch Mk 8 Mod 1; Sylver (48 Aster 30/Aster 15; 2 30mm; 2 Phalanx CIWS; 1 Merlin or 2 Lynxes. Provision for Harpoon Torpedo tubes
Sensors	Radar: Types 1045 (Sampson), 1046 (S1850M), 1047, 1048
	Sonar: Type 2091
Command system	CMS-1
Machinery	Integrated electric propulsion: 2 WR-21 gas turbines, 2 12V200 diesels
	30 knots
	Range: 7,000 nautical miles at 18 knots
Complement	235

Construction programme

The initial requirement was for 12 Type 45s to replace the existing Type 42, but by 2004 this had reduced to eight and then to six in 2008 as the costs of the programme increased. The names chosen not only revived some of those in the previous post-war Daring-class destroyers (*Daring* herself, *Diamond* and *Defender*), but also old cruiser (*Dauntless* and *Dragon*) and battleship (*Duncan*) names. The last ship of the class, HMS *Duncan*, was delivered four months ahead of schedule.

Pendant	Name	Yard	1st steel cut	Launched	Completed
D32	*Daring*	BVT/BAE, Scotstoun, Clyde	28/03/03	01/02/06	23/07/09
D33	*Dauntless*	BVT/BAE, Scotstoun, Clyde	26/08/04	23/01/07	03/06/10
D34	*Diamond*	BVT/BAE, Scotstoun, Clyde	25/02/05	27/11/07	06/05/11
D35	*Dragon*	BVT/BAE, Scotstoun, Clyde	19/12/05	17/11/08	20/04/12
D36	*Defender*	BVT/BAE, Scotstoun, Clyde	31/07/06	21/10/09	21/03/13
D37	*Duncan*	BVT/BAE, Scotstoun, Clyde	26/01/07	11/10/10	26/09/13

OPERATIONAL SERVICE

Initial roles

The first County-class destroyers were capable and striking vessels in a fleet that still had many wartime ships. They were usually attached to carrier groups to provide missile air defence. They were used in a range of duties, which included supporting British land forces in the 'confrontation' with Indonesia in Borneo, the 'Beira' patrol off Mozambique to enforce sanctions on the rebel colonial regime of Rhodesia and the enforcement of the 'innocent right of passage' by vessels in the seas around the Philippines and Indonesia in the late 1960s. County-class vessels were also in attendance during the withdrawal from British bases in the Persian Gulf, Indian Ocean and

South East Asia between 1967 and 1971. Following the Turkish invasion of Cyprus in 1974, *Devonshire* and *Hampshire* helped evacuate British nationals while supporting the commando carrier HMS *Hermes*. During the Iran–Iraq War of 1980–88 the Armilla Patrol in the Persian Gulf was established to protect British shipping. The Type 42s were the mainstay of the patrol and the first ship on station was *Coventry* in October 1980.

The Falklands Campaign

In the early hours of 2 April 1982, Argentinian forces invaded the Falkland Islands, a British dependent territory in the South Atlantic. The much smaller island of South Georgia was also invaded. Despite stiff resistance from the small Royal Marine garrison, the islands' defences were overwhelmed and the Governor capitulated at 1.15pm that day, fearing that further resistance would endanger the lives of the Falkland Islanders. The islands had been claimed by Argentina (inheriting a pre-independence Spanish claim) for many years, but domestic factors, including the military government's increasing unpopularity, pushed the Argentine president, General Galtieri, into ordering the invasion as a populist measure. The population of the islands was predominantly of British background and had long been in favour of remaining under British rule.

The British government had been unprepared for such actions, but quickly ordered the assembling of a naval task force to head south, and if necessary retake the islands. This was backed up by a United Nations resolution which demanded the immediate withdrawal of Argentinian forces. Rear Admiral

HMS *Diamond*: aft of the Mk 8 4.5-inch gun is the raised superstructure containing the 48 Sylver launchers. Atop the foremast is the Sampson radar in its distinctive 'golf ball' rotating covering. On the mainmast is the S1850M air-search radar with its black rotating array. (MoD/Open Government Licence v3.0)

F

HMS *GLAMORGAN* IN THE FALKLANDS

In the early hours of the morning of 12 June 1982, HMS *Glamorgan* had just completed four hours of naval gunfire support, firing 145 shells, to 45 Commando Royal Marines as they fought to take Two Sisters ridge on the route to Port Stanley. The Task Force was aware that the Argentinians had transferred some of their naval Exocet canisters and missiles to land-based trailers, and this threat meant that *Glamorgan* needed to keep her distance from the shoreline. Unfortunately the Argentinians had sited their launchers nearer to *Glamorgan* than had been anticipated – an Exocet was launched at the destroyer as she withdrew from the gun line and was leaving action stations. The missile was detected with only two minutes' notice. She fired a Sea Cat at the approaching missile, but it failed to make its target. Meanwhile, the ship's navigator had instigated a sharp turn to starboard with the aim of not only producing a narrower target but also increasing the chance of a glancing blow rather than the full impact which had mortally damaged *Sheffield* five weeks before. The turn was not completed, but the 14-degree heel produced by such an emergency turn at 25 knots meant that when the Exocet hit, it did not impact on the hull, but exploded against the temporarily angled deck while the ship turned. The missile exploded to the port side of the hangar, throwing the Sea Cat launcher into the air, collapsing the hangar doors and knocking a hole into the deck below where the ship's galley was located. Fires started in the hangar and in the galley and the ship started the fight for her survival. If the fires had reached the Sea Slug missile magazine below, the ship would, no doubt, have been lost. Effective firefighting ensured that this did not occur, but the amount of water needed to dowse the flames soon led to stability problems which could have capsized the warship. Luckily, one of the crew members fighting the fires below decks had the foresight to remove the plugs which allowed the water – which was as deep as 5 feet in places – to even out across the lower decks. The ship had been saved, but at a terrible cost. Thirteen crew members lost their lives, including many members of the flight crew and several of those in the galley. *Glamorgan* was the first warship to survive an Exocet attack and live to fight another day.

HMS *Sheffield* at the US naval base at Diego Garcia in the Indian Ocean, February 1982. Only a month later she would be diverted to join the task force heading to the South Atlantic. (Nathalmad/CC-BY-3.0)

'Sandy' Woodward, the Flag Officer of the First Flotilla, was chosen as commander of the task force. He had been leading the Royal Navy's annual Springtrain exercise in the Mediterranean, which included *Antrim*, *Glamorgan*, *Coventry* and *Glasgow* as well as three frigates. *Sheffield*, which had been on a long deployment east of Suez, was also attached to the group, and the vessels headed south to the island of Ascension, another British territory, 3,800 miles to the north of the Falklands. These vessels arrived at Ascension between 10 and 12 April and were joined by the two carriers and additional vessels on 16 and 17 April.

Antrim, along with the frigate *Plymouth* and the Royal Fleet Auxiliary tanker *Tidespring* were the ships selected for the operation to liberate South Georgia, codenamed Operation *Paraquet*. *Antrim* took on board 150 Royal Marines and 70 SAS who would conduct the landings, using the three Wessex helicopters available to the force. Two Wessex helicopters were lost in poor conditions on the Fortuna Glacier, but the SAS reconnaissance group on board and the aircrew were rescued by *Antrim*'s Wessex. The Argentinian submarine *Santa Fe* was known to be in the area, and she was spotted on the surface on 25 April by the same Wessex which damaged her with depth charges; she was then attacked by other aircraft in the force. *Santa Fe* reached Grytviken, South Georgia, heavily damaged and completely disabled. Royal Marines were then landed later that day by *Antrim*'s Wessex and the other ships' Wasp helicopters following a naval bombardment. Argentinian forces ashore surrendered before being engaged by the landing force. The first part of the operation in the South Atlantic had ended successfully, with not a little luck on the side of the British forces.

The main task force was enforcing a Maritime Exclusion Zone that had been established around the Falklands. The threat from the Argentine Navy was neutralized by the sinking of the cruiser *General Belgrano* by the submarine HMS *Conqueror* on 2 May. The shock of this loss forced the Argentine Navy off the open seas for the rest of the war. On 3 May, the Argentinian patrol vessel, the *Sobral*, was damaged by Sea Skuas from *Glasgow*'s Lynx helicopter.

The next day, 4 May, the Argentinian Navy launched an attack on the British task force with its land-based Super-Etendards, armed with the sea-skimming Exocet missile. Owing to the lack of an airborne early warning aircraft, which had been withdrawn from naval service in 1978 following the scrapping of the navy's last fixed-wing aircraft carrier, HMS *Ark Royal*, the three Type 42 destroyers, *Sheffield*, *Coventry* and *Glasgow*, with their long-range air-search radars were placed at the head of the task force as radar pickets to detect any air threat and engage it with their Sea Dart missiles. This placed these vessels in a vulnerable position: they would be the first targets seen by the enemy and probably the first to be engaged. None of these original Type 42s would be in the task force by the time of the Argentinian surrender: two had been lost to air attacks and the third withdrawn to Ascension to repair heavy bomb damage. On 4 May it was to be *Sheffield*'s fate to be targeted.

The task force had suffered from a number of false contacts over the previous days – Argentine Mirage IIIs had similar radar signatures to the Exocet-armed Super-Etendards – and intelligence reports had doubted that the newly delivered Exocet missiles were even usable, given the recent withdrawal of support from their French manufacturer. The two Harriers assigned to combat air patrol had been diverted south to search for Argentine warships. In addition, the Argentine pilots, having practised against their navy's own Type 42s, were aware of one of the weaknesses of these ships' air-search radar (the Type 965): it was not proficient at locating low-flying targets. The pilots, therefore, flew as low as possible. A radar contact was made by *Glasgow*, the Type 42 in the centre of the picket line, which reported the rapid approach of Argentine aircraft. *Sheffield* was using her satellite communications system at the time, which meant she could not pick up the radar emissions from the aircraft. Her anti-air warfare officer was not in the operations room at that moment and *Glasgow*'s message was only partly picked up. Both the operations rooms of the aircraft carrier *Invincible* and *Sheffield* believed that the contacts were Mirages on a standard bombing run rather than Super-Etendards armed with Exocets. *Glasgow* then reported the launch of two missiles from the aircraft and took countermeasures by launching metal 'chaff' into the air to confuse the radars of the missiles. One missile passed into the sea soon after launch, but the chaff might well have inadvertently diverted one of the Exocets towards *Sheffield*, although it is just as likely that she was the first ship onto which the missile's radar guidance locked. By the time *Sheffield* was fully aware of the real situation, it was only 15 seconds to impact: too late for any countermeasures to be taken.

At 2:03pm the missile hit on the starboard side amidships. The warhead of the missile probably never exploded, but the impact and the spread of unspent missile fuel immediately started fires in the centre of the ship. The placing of the impact disabled the ship's war fighting capacity immediately, and fire-fighting teams could not control the blaze. Such was the surprise of the impact that it was thought for some time by other vessels in the task force that *Sheffield* had been torpedoed. As the fires began to approach the Sea Dart magazine, Captain Salt made the order to abandon ship and the Type 42 was left to burn herself out. Attempts were made to tow the burnt-out hull to Ascension, but she foundered in bad weather on 10 May. Twenty men died, and the loss of *Sheffield* made clear the seriousness of the conflict to the British government and public.

The loss of *Sheffield* demonstrated that the Type 42s were vulnerable to sea-skimming missiles aimed directly at them. Although there were doubts back in the UK, Admiral Woodward trialled the concept of pairing the two remaining Type 42 pickets with the two modern

HMS *Sheffield* on fire after being hit by an Exocet missile. The warhead probably did not explode, but unexpended fuel from the missile and the speed of impact caused a series of fires to break out that the crew were unable to control. (Imperial War Museum, FKD 66)

HMS *Cardiff* with a Sea Dart missile on its launcher, seen from the bridge. The impact of the South Atlantic weather can be seen in the rust on the launcher. Note its bulbous rocket booster at the bottom of the missile. (Kenneth Ian Griffiths/CC-BY-SA 3.0)

Type 22 frigates, which were armed with the state-of-the-art Sea Wolf point-defence system. Sea Wolf was designed to defend the ship on which it was carried, and it was hoped that operating a Type 42 and Type 22 in close formation as a '42/22 combo' would give the Type 42 the self-defence she needed to fulfil her picket role and use her Sea Darts to intercept missiles or aircraft approaching other vessels. The Type 22's surveillance radar did not have the low-flying blind spot of the Type 42's Type 965 radar, which would also help the vessels to coordinate their joint air defence. Luring Argentine aircraft out to attack the combo could in effect produce a missile trap where both Sea Dart and Sea Wolf could perform to their strengths.

The first test of the 42/22 combo had mixed results. On 12 May *Glasgow* and HMS *Brilliant*, operating off East Falkland, were attacked by two waves of four Argentine Skyhawk jets. In the first wave, *Brilliant*'s Sea Wolf knocked two Skyhawks out of the sky, while a third crashed into the sea evading attack. Unfortunately, the Sea Dart system suffered a fault just before launch and was unable to operate. The second wave of Skyhawks managed to strike home after both the Sea Wolf and Sea Dart systems malfunctioned. One bomb from the second wave of Skyhawks hit *Glasgow*. It did not explode, but passed straight through the ship, causing flooding and damage. *Glasgow* was withdrawn from picket duty for repairs and was later sent home when it became clear that the repairs could not be fully completed in the South Atlantic. *Glasgow* might have left the conflict zone, but the arrival of additional vessels to supplement the task force brought *Exeter* on 19 May, and *Cardiff* and *Bristol* on 23 May. *Exeter*, the first Batch 2 ship, had the advantage of being equipped with the new Type 1022 radar that suffered from none of the low-flying blind spots of the other Type 42s.

Meanwhile, plans were being finalized for the landing of troops to retake the islands. It had been decided that the landing force would disembark at San Carlos Bay on the west side of East Falkland. It was hoped that this

G **HMS *GLOUCESTER* IN THE GULF**

As part of one of the diversionary actions during the 1990–91 Gulf War to convince Iraqi forces that an amphibious landing was imminent, the US battleship *Missouri*, along with a force of British minesweepers, and escorted by the frigate USS *Jarrett* and by HMS *Gloucester*, approached the Kuwaiti coast. The *Missouri* commenced shore bombardment operations with its enormous World War II-vintage guns, while the minesweepers cleared channels for the other ships, suggesting the approach of amphibious warfare vessels. This operation was a success in that it fooled the Iraqis into keeping troops facing the sea to repel an assault that never came, which enabled Coalition land forces to encircle them. It also provoked the Iraqis into launching two Chinese-made Silkworm anti-ship missiles at the naval force. *Gloucester*'s systems detected the Silkworms as they crossed from land to sea, and only two minutes from the *Missouri*. After some nervous seconds trying to detect whether the radar blips were friend or foe, the *Gloucester*, which had been facing eastwards, manoeuvred into position to allow her Sea Dart launcher to bear. The *Jarrett* and *Missouri* launched chaff metal decoys to confuse the one remaining Silkworm (the other crashed harmlessly into the sea) and placed their Phalanx last-ditch missile defence guns on automatic. *Gloucester* launched two Sea Darts at the target and within seconds one had found its target: from the bridge of the *Jarrett*, and through the smog of burning oil wells on the coast, a huge fireball was seen behind the *Gloucester*. The Silkworm by the time it was destroyed had flown past the *Missouri*, but it was, nonetheless, a significant achievement: the world's first operational missile-on-missile kill at sea had just occurred, only two minutes after the missile had been detected on *Gloucester*'s radar.

would not be expected by the Argentinians, who would presume that a landing would occur close to the capital Port Stanley. To encourage this perception, HMS *Glamorgan* was assigned to lead Operation *Tornado*, bombarding the area near Stanley and sending dummy signals, in addition to other activities as a deception. The real invasion – Operation *Sutton* – would be led by HMS *Antrim*, which would lead the escort force

HMS *Coventry* listing heavily and soon to capsize. The three bombs caused flooding across more than three watertight sections of the warship, and given that it took only 20 minutes for the ship to capsize, it is a testament to effective abandon-ship procedures that only 19 lost their lives. (Imperial War Museum, FKD 1265)

protecting the assault ships *Fearless* and *Intrepid* and the troop carrier *Canberra* and a number of other vessels. *Glamorgan*'s deception operation helped to achieve the desired effect and the Argentinians were taken by surprise by the landing and even then took some time to understand that San Carlos Bay was the main landing site and not itself a feint. However, after the initial confusion, it was quickly realized that there were considerable Royal Navy forces in San Carlos Bay, so Argentinian air-force attacks started in the early afternoon after the landings.

Argentine air force Daggers undertook the first raid and concentrated on the largest warships escorting the landing force, HMS *Antrim* and HMS *Broadsword*. *Broadsword*'s Sea Wolf managed to down a Dagger, but *Antrim* was hit and partly disabled by a bomb that had not exploded, and with her Sea Cat system out of action she was partly defenceless. The unexploded bomb was removed, but the damage was sufficient for *Antrim* to be withdrawn from San Carlos Bay. The total number of Argentine air-force aircraft used that day to attack the landing force had been 45. Ten had been destroyed, but the Argentinians had managed to destroy one frigate (HMS *Ardent*) and damage four other warships including *Antrim*. However, the Argentinians had focused on the warships, drawing their fire from the vulnerable troopships and thereby ensuring that the landing itself was successful: all troops were brought ashore with very few casualties and a beachhead quickly established.

Once the land force was ashore, the amphibious commanders, Brigadier Thompson and Commodore Clapp, argued for more effective air defence by bringing the carriers closer to enable their Harriers (armed with the effective Sidewinder missile) to have more time and fuel to patrol over East Falkland. Woodward was unwilling to risk the carriers, but as a compromise, he was

A diagram showing the nature of the bomb damage to *Coventry* that led to her sinking. The diagram shows the entry points of the three bombs: the first entered below the ship's computer room and operations room, the second just aft through store rooms, and the third entered the gas turbine intakes and exploded inside the Olympus turbine room. (MoD Naval Historical Branch)

willing to re-establish the 42/22 combo with *Coventry* and *Broadsword* off the north-west of the Falklands to intercept Argentinian aircraft before they got to San Carlos. On 24 May the combo had successes in directing attacks by Harriers onto Argentinian aircraft, but the heaviest challenge came on 25 May, Argentinian Independence Day. *Coventry* had been successful in intercepting Argentinian Skyhawks returning from raids on San Carlos, destroying two with Sea Dart. A third raid that day, approaching from behind the land, and therefore making it more difficult for the ships' radars to obtain targets, managed to breach the defences of the combo. Initially, *Broadsword*'s Sea Wolf targeting radar could not lock onto a target because of land clutter behind. When eventually it could, the line of fire was obscured by *Coventry*, which was making evasive manoeuvres to present a smaller target to the aircraft. Sea Wolf was not fired and three bombs penetrated *Coventry's* hull disabling her immediately and causing flooding, which soon destabilized the ship. The crew abandoned ship and *Coventry* capsized an hour after she had been hit. Nineteen crewmembers died. On the same day, the Argentinian Navy launched an Exocet attack on the carrier task group, hitting the *Atlantic Conveyor*, a merchant vessel converted into an aircraft and stores transport. The loss of her Chinook troop helicopters was particularly keenly felt by the land forces. For naval losses this was the worst day for the task force. Of those that had survived so far, many vessels were either damaged or developing defects from such a long time on operations far from bases. However, 25 May would also prove to be the turning point in the naval campaign. Other attacks were made, but with decreasing regularity and with perhaps a reduced willingness to press them home.

The last attack on the task force occurred on 30 May. Two Super Etendard attacked first. A single Exocet was launched and headed towards a frigate in the task force but it was decoyed by chaff and fell into the sea. Next came an attack by four Skyhawks. One was destroyed by Sea Dart from *Exeter*, another was destroyed by small-arms fire and the remaining two released their bombs without effect. Intelligence was beginning to be picked up that the Argentinians had adapted ship-launched Exocets for use on trailers, and which could therefore be deployed from shore. *Exeter* appears to have had a lucky escape, as the first attempt to launch two Exocets at a bombarding frigate resulted in a miss and one missile stuck in its launcher. As British land forces consolidated their position on East Falkland, on 6 June a tragic accident occurred: a Gazelle helicopter carrying two members of 5 Infantry Brigade signals staff was destroyed by Sea Darts from *Cardiff* off Fitzroy: a message had not got through to *Cardiff* quickly enough that the aircraft would be flying. On the early morning of 12 June *Glamorgan* provided gunfire support for the advance of British forces along the line of Mount Longdon and Wireless Ridge towards Port Stanley. After firing 261 shells that night, and beginning her departure from the gun line, she was hit by a trailer-launched Exocet from land but kept the fire under control, preventing it spreading to the Sea Slug magazine. *Glamorgan* returned to the task force operational but having suffered 28 casualties including 13 dead. On 13 June the Argentinians made their last concerted air attack on British forces. These attacks had little impact, but *Cardiff* did destroy an Argentinian Canberra on its return from a bombing raid on British forces on Mount Kent. As the Parachute Regiment and Royal Marines reached Stanley, the resistance of the Argentinian Army crumbled and near midnight on 14 June, General Menendez surrendered his troops.

The recapture of the Falklands would have been impossible without the use of British naval power, and British destroyers played a significant part in the operations. The Type 42s were at the core of the air defence of the task force. Sea Dart had performed creditably in certain circumstances, but more significantly after the conflict the importance of naval air defence was recognized and planning began for the eventual replacement of the Type 42s. The two

The Argentinian Navy Super-Etendard 3-A-204 in a hangar and showing her weapon fit. This aircraft's Exocets hit and destroyed the *Atlantic Conveyor*. (Martin Otero/CC-BY-2.5)

This photograph shows the damage to *Glamorgan's* hangar after the fires had been put out. Her port Sea Cat launcher had disappeared, the helicopter in the hangar had been destroyed and the hole in the deck that the missile punched can be seen clearly. (Imperial War Museum, FKD 75)

HMS *Cardiff*, 1997. This photo shows the ship without the distinctive radomes of the Type 909 tracker radars. The radomes were necessary to protect the radar from the weather and salt water. (Imperial War Museum, CT 2396)

Counties in the conflict had been in the heat of many of the battles, their size and gun armament making them useful vessels for shore bombardment and for leading particular missions, such as the recapture of South Georgia and leading the amphibious ships into San Carlos.

The 1990–91 Gulf War

On 2 August 1990 Iraqi forces invaded and occupied Kuwait. A United States-led coalition supported by United Nations Security Council resolutions assembled land, air and naval forces to liberate Kuwait. The United Kingdom's participation in this campaign was codenamed Operation *Granby*.

On the invasion of Kuwait, the British Armilla patrol consisted of two frigates and the Type 42 destroyer *York*. In September, *York* and the two original frigates were relieved by four vessels: the Type 42s *Gloucester* and *Cardiff* and two Type 22 frigates *Brazen* and *London*. One of the major roles of the British naval contingent was to enforce a maritime blockade on Iraq, by stopping and searching vessels in the Gulf. The Type 42 destroyers also worked closely with the US carrier groups in the air-defence role. In February further vessels arrived: the Type 42s *Manchester* and *Exeter* and two more Type 22s.

In order to ensure control of the sea off the coast of occupied Kuwait and Iraq, offensive operations against Iraqi naval vessels – mostly fast attack craft or patrol vessels – began early in the campaign. Tactics were developed jointly by US and British forces whereby the radar on US SH-60B helicopters gave target information to Royal Navy shipborne Lynx helicopters, which undertook attacks using the Sea Skua anti-ship missile system. This joint approach would prove to be very successful. The first major engagement started on 29 January when 15 small Iraqi warships were sent into Saudi coastal waters, perhaps to land forces to support a ground attack on al-Khafji. Three vessels were sunk and many more damaged. The total success of this operation was demonstrated by the Iraqi naval command issuing orders to the surviving vessels to flee and seek sanctuary in Iran. *Gloucester* and *Cardiff*'s Lynx helicopters notched up seven confirmed Sea Skua hits in this two-day action. Further successful attacks on 8 and 9 February against the few remaining Iraqi small craft brave enough to go to sea were achieved by the Lynxes of *Cardiff* and *Manchester*. *Gloucester*, escorting the US battleship *Missouri*, achieved the very first destruction of an anti-ship missile by an air-defence missile, when an Iraqi Silkworm missile was destroyed by her Sea Dart on 25 February.

HMS *Diamond* escorting a merchant vessel, which is carrying Syrian chemical weapons for disposal, as part of Operation *Recsyr* in February 2014. (MoD/Open Government Licence v3.0)

The British naval contribution to the sea war to liberate Kuwait was significant operationally: Type 42s had not only successfully defended major vessels against missile attack, they had also – through their Sea Skua-armed Lynx helicopters – been one of the most important contributors to the operations to destroy Iraqi naval capabilities.

Operational deployments since 1991

The deployments of the Type 42 destroyers in the post-Cold War period demonstrate the worldwide nature of Britain's maritime commitments. To take HMS *Glasgow* as an example: she was deployed to the Persian Gulf and Indian Ocean twice, first in 1991–92, just missing out on involvement in Operation *Granby*, and then again in 1993–94 to enforce sanctions against Iraq. In 1992 she deployed as part of the first NATO Standing Naval Force in the Mediterranean, attending the inauguration of this multinational deployable squadron. In 1995–96 *Glasgow* was deployed to the Adriatic to enforce the UN embargo on Yugoslavia, and then she was involved in US–UK naval exercises off the US coast. In 2000–01 she was deployed to the South Atlantic, but she spent most of her deployment supporting the stabilization of Sierra Leone following UN and British intervention to restore the legitimate government. Her final major deployment in 2003 was on a Falklands patrol, where she also gave further

HMS *Edinburgh* fires the last Sea Dart missiles in 2013 just before her decommissioning. The missile had started development in 1962 and entered service in the Royal Navy in 1973. (MoD/Open Government Licence v3.0)

support to Sierra Leone stabilization. In the last months of her final commission, she visited her home town for the last time and attended the Dutch 'Navy Days'. She was decommissioned in January 2005 after 26 years' service in the Royal Navy.

In the 2003 Gulf War *Edinburgh*, *Liverpool* and *York* all deployed to the Gulf in support of HMS *Ark Royal* and HMS *Ocean* as part of Operation *Telic*. *Ark Royal* and *Ocean* acted as amphibious vessels, landing 3 Commando Brigade on the Al Faw peninsula, and the Type 42s acted as their air-defence escorts. From 2003 the surviving Type 42s were deployed on a range of exercises and operations internationally, including as guard ships in the West Indies and as part of patrols of the Falklands. During the Libya campaign of 2011, *Liverpool* bombarded rocket batteries ashore and directed aircraft during the air campaign while *York* evacuated people from Benghazi and delivered aid. The arrival into service of the Type 45s heralded a new era for British guided missile destroyers, and *Daring*'s first few years were spent on trials and testing her new air-defence capabilities. In 2014 *Diamond* was involved in operations to support the destruction of Syrian chemical weapons and *Duncan* was present at the Cardiff NATO summit of that year.

The fates of the British guided missile destroyers

Name	Paid off	Fate
Devonshire	1978	Potential sale to Egypt fell through in 1980. Expended as target ship in 1985
Hampshire	1976	Scrapped in 1976
Kent	1980	Harbour training ship in 1980, accommodation ship at Portsmouth, then later accommodation and static training ship for Sea Cadet Corps. Replaced by *Bristol* in 1993 and scrapped. Plans to sell to Chile to provide spares for the Batch 2 vessels were dropped
London	1980	Sold to Pakistan in 1982 as *Babur*. Sea Slug removed in 1984 and became Sea Cadet training ship. Withdrawn from service in 1993
Glamorgan	1986	Sold to Chile in 1986 as *Latorre*. Withdrawn from service in 1998
Fife	1987	In 1986 converted to Sea Cadet training ship. Sold to Chile in 1987 as *Blanco Encalada*. Sea Slug removed, flight deck extended aft and hangar for two helicopters installed in 1988. Withdrawn from service in 2003
Antrim	1984	Sold to Chile in 1984 as *Almirante Cochrane*. Modernized as per *Blanco Encalada* (ex-*Fife*) 1994. Withdrawn from service in 2006
Norfolk	1982	Sold to Chile in 1982 as *Capitán Prat*. Withdrawn from service in 2006
Bristol	1991	Dartmouth training ship 1987–91. Static Sea Cadet training ship at Portsmouth from 1993. Still extant
Sheffield	–	Hit by Exocet missile 04/05/1982, sank under tow 10/05/1982
Birmingham	11/1999	Cannibalized for spares, towed away for scrap 10/2000
Cardiff	08/2005	Towed for scrapping 11/2008
Coventry	–	Hit by three bombs 25/05/1982, capsized and later sank
Newcastle	01/2005	Towed for scrapping 11/2008
Glasgow	01/2005	Towed for scrapping 12/2008
Exeter	06/2009	Towed for scrapping 09/2011
Southampton	03/2009	Towed for scrapping 10/2011
Nottingham	03/2010	Towed for scrapping 10/2011
Liverpool	03/2012	Towed for scrapping 10/2014
Manchester	02/2011	Towed for scrapping 11/2014
Gloucester	06/2011	Awaiting scrap, Portsmouth
Edinburgh	06/2013	Awaiting scrap, Portsmouth
York	09/2012	Awaiting scrap, Portsmouth

BIBLIOGRAPHY

Brown, David, *The Royal Navy and the Falklands War*, London, Guild Publication (1987)

Brown, D. K. and Moore, George, *Rebuilding the Royal Navy*, London, Chatham (2003)

Bush, Steve, *British Warships and Auxiliaries*, Liskeard, Maritime (various editions)

Elliott, Toby, *Royal Navy Task Force 321.1: A Gulf Record*, Connexions, Dubai (1991)

Fox, Robert, *Iraq Campaign 2003: Royal Navy and Royal Marines*, London, Agenda (2003)

Freedman, Lawrence, *The Official History of the Falklands Campaign, Vol. II*, Basingstoke, Routledge (2005)

Friedman, Norman, *The Postwar Naval Revolution*, London, Conway Maritime Press (1986)

Friedman, Norman, *British Destroyers and Frigates*, London, Chatham (2006)

Friedman, Norman, (ed.), *World Naval Weapon Systems*, Annapolis, MD, Naval Institute Press (various edns)

Gardiner, Robert (ed.), *Navies in the Nuclear Age*, London, Conway Maritime Press (1993)

Hampshire, Edward, *From East of Suez to the Eastern Atlantic* Farnham, Ashgate (2013)

Hart Dyke, David, *Four Weeks in May: The Loss of HMS* Coventry – *A Captain's Story*, London, Atlantic (2007)

Hill, J. R., *Air Defence at Sea*, Shepperton, Ian Allan (1988)

Inskip, Ian, *Ordeal by Exocet: HMS* Glamorgan *and the Falklands War, 1982*, London, Chatham (2002)

Jane's Fighting Ships, Coulsdon (various editions)

McCart, Neil, *County Class Guided Missile Destroyers*, Liskeard, Maritime (2014)

Marriott, Leo, *Type 42*, Shepperton, Ian Allan (1985)

Marriott, Leo, *British Destroyers since 1945*, Shepperton, Ian Allan (1989)

Pokrant, Marvin, *Desert Storm at Sea: What the Navy Really Did*, Westport, CT, Greenwood Press (1999)

Prezelin, Bernard (ed., French edn), (A. D. Baker, ed., US edn), *Combat Fleets of the World*, Éditions Maritimes et d'Outre-Mer; Annapolis, MD, Naval Institute Press (various edns)

Waters, Conrad, 'HMS *Daring*' in *Seaforth World Naval Review 2010*, ed. Conrad Waters, Barnsley, Seaforth (2009)

www.countyclassdestroyers.co.uk
www.type42association.co.uk
www.royalnavy.mod.uk
MoD Archive

INDEX

References to illustrations are shown in **bold**.
Plates are shown with page locators in brackets.